SOLVE IT WITH SALT

SOLVE IT WITH
SALT

110 Surprising and Ingenious Household Uses for

TABLE SALT

PATTY MOOSBRUGGER

THREE RIVERS PRESS

Published by Three River Press, a division of Crown Publishers, Inc., 201 East 50th Street, New York, New York 10022. Member of the Crown Publishing Group.

Random House, Inc. New York, Toronto, London, Sydney, Auckland
www.randomhouse.com/

Three Rivers Press and colophon are trademarks of Crown Publishers, Inc.
Design by Howard P. Johnson
Printed in the United States of America

Library of Congress Cataloging-in-Publication Data

Moosbrugger, Patty.
    Solve it with salt : 110 surprising and ingenious household uses for table salt / Patty Moosbrugger. — 1st ed.
        p.   cm.
    Includes bibliographical references and index.
    1. Home economics.   2. Salt.   1. House cleaning.   I. Title.
    TX158.M66   1998
    640'.41—dc21   97-32775
                                                                   CIP

ISBN 0-609-80234-8 (pbk.)

10 9 8 7 6 5 4 3 2 1

First Edition

Author's Note

The author has included cautions and general guidelines for using salt in this book. However, each individual, fabric, or material may react differently to a particular suggested use. For this reason, the author cannot assume responsibility for personal or property damage resulting from the use of the suggestions found here. It is recommended that before you begin to use any suggestion, you read the directions carefully. With respect to the use of salt on any fabric or material, test it first in a small, inconspicuous place. If you have any questions or concerns regarding the safety or health effects of any suggestions, consult first with a physician or other appropriate professional.

Acknowledgments

Thank you, above all, to Chris Hornsby, whose assistance and input helped shape the book and whose patience and prodding helped me finish the book on time.

Thanks too to Wendy Hubbert, whose idea this book was and who had enough faith in me to trust me with the project.

Many thanks as well to Mary Quiroz, who discovered some amazing sources for me, and to PJ Dempsey, who took over the project with great enthusiasm and helped guide me through the editorial process.

Contents

A BRIEF
HISTORY
OF SALT

*T*he ordinary shaker of salt that you can find in every kitchen or restaurant today is something so commonplace that it's hard to imagine the important role that salt has played throughout history. With the advent of modern mining techniques, salt has become an inexpensive and readily available commodity that is taken for granted by most people. But in older times wars were fought over salt, and huge taxes were also levied on it. In some places, salt was in such high demand that it was minted into coins that were as valuable as gold and functioned as the basic currency for ancient civilizations.

"Table salt" is a chemically simple combination of two components, sodium and chlorine. The basic components of salt are, by themselves, potentially dangerous. Sodium will ignite immediately if it comes into contact with water, and chlorine is poisonous if ingested. In combination, though, the two elements form sodium chloride, commonly known as salt. In the body, salt is as important to humans as water or air. It helps maintain the normal volume of blood in the body and also helps keep the correct balance of water in and around the cells and tissues. Salt plays an important part in the digestion of food and is essential in making the heart beat correctly. It is also necessary for the formation and proper function of nerve fibers, which carry impulses to and from the brain. Even as infants in the womb, salt was essential to our development. Amniotic fluid, which surrounds us in the womb, has the same amount of salt in it as the oceans that surround the planet.

Across the globe, salt has been of vital importance to many economies, and from ancient to modern times, salt deposits have been important sources of economic wealth for the areas in which they lie. Today, the vast salt deposits across the earth provide the mineral in unlimited amounts. The sea itself holds enough salt to feed our current consumption level for thousands of years, but ancient man had little access to salt. Rising sea levels in the first millennia B.C. and A.D. flooded the coastal salt pans, causing salt famines. Technology wasn't advanced enough to allow drilling, and so those who had access to salt marshes and coastal salt pools used this to their advantage by either hoarding the salt for themselves and their people or by trading it off for its worth in gold—in many cases the weight in salt was equal to the weight in gold.

So important was salt across the globe in ancient times that it was a major method of exchange. People were willing to trade items of great value for the precious mineral. In Africa, Tibet, and Borneo salt was used as money, and Roman soldiers were paid part of their wages in salt. This Roman salt payment was called a *salarium,* the very word from which we have derived our modern equivalent, *salary.* In America, the first European settlers brought salt with them and used it as a valuable trading tool with the Indians, who would trade food, furs, and even land for the precious mineral.

In the Sudan, some tribes had gold but no salt, but in the Sahara region, which lies north of the Sudan, salt existed in abundance in large deposits laid bare by the shifting desert sands. Between these regions lay the famed city of Timbuktu, the embarkation point of the medieval gold caravans to the Mediterranean. At a secret trading place beyond Timbuktu, Moorish merchants traveled with their huge slabs of salt to trade for gold. When they arrived at the trading site, the merchants would beat upon drums to signal their arrival, set down their piles of salt, and quietly withdraw. Emerging from the mines, the gold diggers placed piles of gold next to the piles of salt and withdrew, as the salt bearers had earlier done. The Moors then returned, and if the trade was satisfactory, they would beat their drums to signal the end of the trade. But more likely, the Moors would detract some of their salt, again retreat, and await the ensuing judgment of the gold bearers. This could go on back and forth for many tries before the drums were again beaten to signal the end of the trading.

The trading of salt, in fact, led to some of the first major trading routes throughout the world. One of the oldest roads stretches across the Sahara from the oasis at Bilma in West Africa to the seaports on the coast. At Bilma a salt crust formed on the marshes. This was broken up, raked together, packed on camels' backs, carried to the ports, and from there shipped to Europe and Asia. Caravans of camels still carry salt across the vast Sahara even today.

In Italy, one of the oldest salt-trading routes, the Via Salaria (salt way), was used to carry salt from Ostia, near Rome, to the northeast. Today it is one of Italy's major highways.

In England, the road from Chester to London began as a path over which salt from the Cheshire mines was brought to the port on the Thames, and from there was shipped across the channel to Gaul, now France. In the United States, mule caravans carried salt from what is now Alamogordo, New Mexico, to the silver mines of Sonora, Mexico. U.S. Highway 70 now follows that very salt trail. And the Erie Canal was dug in part to transport the salt from the great mines in Syracuse, New York.

Not only did roads grow up to ease access to salt trading, but whole cities were also founded along these routes to shelter caravans. In addition, cities grew up around the production of salt. In England, towns with names ending in *wich,* such as Norwich and Greenwich, owe their beginnings to salt. *Wich* is the Saxon word for a "a place where salt is dug." In Germany and Austria these towns have either *salz* or *hall* in their names.

Throughout the world, the trading of salt developed the landscape, and as the trading of salt grew in importance, governments began to see the promise in regulating that trade and regulating the flow of such a valuable resource. This led to wars, to taxation, and in some cases to mass death from the deprivation that resulted from the wars over salt.

As early as 250 B.C. the Carthaginians went to war over salt. They fought the Romans and Greeks to win control over the important salt-producing centers on the Mediterranean and Adriatic coasts as well as to control the trade routes used for transporting salt. Unfortunately, the Carthaginians didn't win that war, and the very salt they fought to gain control of was used to destroy them. The Romans plowed salt into all of their land to prevent anything from growing there.

Under the ancien régime, the French people had to buy salt from royal depots. When the king needed more money, he simply increased the amount of salt that each person must buy. But this governmental control over salt eventually turned on the French government. The hated salt tax, the *gabelle,* was one of the many causes of the French Revolution.

In history's ugly way of repeating itself, the French salt tax was revived fifteen years after the revolution by Napoleon, who also must have ended up regretting his association with the essential mineral. Salt starvation decimated his troops in their retreat from Moscow, lowering their resistance to disease. Disease spread throughout the troop lines, and thousands died.

Even the American Revolution found cause to fight over salt. Though some of the colonies were producing their own salt by the time the revolution occurred, a great deal of the salt consumed in America was still imported from England. When the war began, the British naturally cut off the supply and went to work trying to seize what saltworks they could.

Starting in Lake Onondaga, New York, the British captured and destroyed a vast salt-producing facility, and from there they moved on down the coast, capturing and destroying as many saltworks as they could find. In New Jersey, the British destroyed several small salteries and burned them to the ground. In Philadelphia, there was an incident much like the great Boston Tea Party where three shiploads of salt were seized and dumped into the Delaware River. When hundreds died in Philadelphia that next winter, the London newspapers triumphantly declared their salt dumping a success.

Throughout the war, the scarcity of salt was badly felt across America as the people became weaker and much more vulnerable to infection. Having felt the effects of such scarcity, the newly independent country was determined to create a system of saltworks that they could rely on.

Salt conflicts were not just problems of the ancient past either. Even in the twentieth century they still arise. The unbearable tax on salt in India, imposed by the British during their occupation, was one of the problems that led to the civil disobedience of the people under Mahatma Gandhi, resulting finally in an independent India.

The mining of salt is a rather late invention in most parts of the world. Early man got most of his food in the form of raw or roasted meat, which provides a high salt content. Many ancient tribes also lived close to the sea and would simply wash their vegetables in the seawater to flavor them with salt. When salt deposits were pushed to the surface, salt could simply be scraped free. But as mankind learned agriculture and started to depend on cereals and grains, salt intake decreased, forcing people to use other means of finding salt to add to their diets. People living close to the sea used methods of evaporation to get salt. Others found saltwater deposits and poured the brine over hot coals to separate the salt from the water and then scraped away the salt.

One of the most fantastic of all salt mines, the great Wieliczka salt mine near Kraków, Poland, is literally a world unto itself. In its early days, the mine started out simply as a place to gather salt that was left loose on the surface. Workmen rigged devices that allowed them to hang suspended from the ceiling of the mine, and they simply scraped the salt off the walls, letting it fall into their aprons until they became full. The workers then lowered themselves to the floor of the mine and emptied the contents of their aprons into baskets, which were carried by mules out of the mines.

In the seventeenth century, the miners began to see the walls of the Wieliczka salt mine as material for sculpture and began to create a vast and fantastic world underground. They carved great chapels out of the salt, finely detailed from the large hanging chandeliers down to the candlesticks on the altars that lay below. In other chambers within the mine, ancient legends came to life, depicted in reliefs that covered the walls and told the stories of heroes. The story of Copernicus, the great Polish astronomer, was also told, and throughout the mine beautiful statues can be found in the fantastic subterranean salt mine that descends nine levels below the surface of the earth. This fascinating site can be visited today (see p. 142).

The fortunes that could be created from a profitable salt mine led Claude Nicolas Ledoux, an eighteenth-century French architect, to dream of a grand city that would be built from the money brought in by the royal saltworks at Arc et Senans. He was friends with King Louis XVI, who allowed him to design a dream city that would include grand houses of pleasure and peace, temples dedicated to goddesses, and a dramatic director's house, orna-mented with huge columns and flanked by two enormous salt-drying pavilions. His lavish dream, though, came to an abrupt end as the French Revo-lution began to unfold. He was jailed for his excesses and left to spend his days behind bars, dreaming of the city that salt would have built in the French countryside.

In this century, in Hutchinson, Kansas, a salt mine that is ordinary by most standards is now being used in a new and creative way. Salt's well-known ability to preserve the freshness of meats, fish, and vegetables by the curing process is being put to good use far beneath the flat Kansas earth in the mine at Hutchinson. This mine has been turned into one of the world's biggest warehouses, holding countless priceless treasures and preserving them from the ravages of both time and light. The dry, salty air that fills the cavernous underground ware-house is a perfect preservative for all sorts of things. Classic, rare editions of Hollywood films, essential corporate documents, and unique strains of agricultural products are but a few of the items that can be found in the chambers of the formerly active Hutchinson salt mine. It is also a temporary rest stop for countless wedding gowns and dresses. For a flat fee, the company that operates the old mine-turned-warehouse will store your wedding attire for twenty-one years—just about the time when the next generation will be ready to wear the perfectly preserved vintage dress.

THE IODIZATION OF SALT

*I*odized salt is the most popular type of salt that consumers buy off the supermarket shelf these days. It is bought without even a thought as to what that iodine is doing in our salt. But in 1924, when iodine was first being added to salt, it created quite a stir.

The father of iodized salt is David Marine. Working with a group of researchers, Marine and his colleagues were studying endemic goiter and its prevalence in the United States in the early 1920s, especially in the Great Lakes areas. Because of the results they achieved in showing the effects of iodine in eliminating endemic goiter (also called hyperthyroidism), Marine and his colleagues convinced the Michigan State Medical Society to develop a prevention program using iodized salt. The salt producers cooperated with the plan and started making both iodized and noniodized salt available to consumers in 1924. Furthermore, the salt companies charged the same price for both types of salt, making the widespread use of iodized salt easy to implement. At the same time, a public campaign was started to inform people of the problems with iodine deficiency, and newspapers urged readers to use the new iodized salt.

In 1923 and 1924 Marine and his colleagues conducted a survey of goiter in Michigan and found that 39 percent of the sixty-six thousand students studied had visible enlargement of their thyroids. After the Michigan Program for iodized salt was instituted, follow-ups were conducted in 1928, 1935, and 1951 to evaluate the results. In 1928 alone, there was already a 70 to 75 percent reduction in the cases of endemic goiter. By 1951, the problem was virtually wiped out. The program was such a success that the use of iodized salt spread throughout the country, which almost single-handedly eliminated goiter in the United States.

While iodine deficiency has been eliminated in

the United States and most other developed countries, it is still a serious problem in some of the developing countries of the world. In 1990 it was listed as the top health priority at the World Summit for Children. The Salt Institute of the United States and the European Salt Producers Association are actively working together to try to eradicate this iodine deficiency through the use of iodized salt. As recently as 1997, a major newspaper reported on the prevalence of goiter throughout China due to the lack of iodized salt; Chinese salt companies, it appears, have balked at the cost and the extra work of iodizing salt.

As it turns out, iodine is not the only substance that can be added to salt as an easy means of reaching the majority of the population. In France, Mexico, and Switzerland, fluoride is added to salt to prevent dental problems. In Egypt, salt is fortified with iron.

The paper that this book is printed on was bleached with salt, one of the many uses of salt that affect our everyday lives.

SALT SUPERSTITIONS

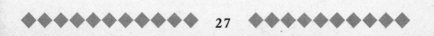

*H*ave a look in the massive dictionary of superstitions and you'll see that salt takes up pages of space. Salt, in fact, has played a part in many superstitions since at least the writing of the Old Testament in the Bible, and other evidence suggests that these superstitions date back to the beginning of the use of salt in prehistoric times. From insuring good health for a newborn child to sending the dead on a straight path to heaven, salt plays some superstitious role in almost every ritual imaginable.

Because of salt's historical importance and its powerful place among early peoples, it was often thought to have magical qualities. After all, it preserved food from going bad, and it did keep people healthy and cure the ill. It is therefore no surprise that salt became associated with superstitions.

One of the most common superstitions about salt says that if you accidentally spill salt, be careful! Spilled salt means bad luck. Unless, of course, you throw a pinch of salt over your left shoulder. This superstition actually dates back as far as 3500 B.C. Because salt was so valuable, spilling the precious commodity was tantamount to bad luck. The practice of nullifying that bad luck by tossing salt over the shoulder was practiced by the ancient Sumerians, the Egyptians, the Assyrians, and later the Greeks. One tradition has it that good spirits stand behind a person's right shoulder, and bad spirits behind his left. Thus, a few grains of salt tossed over the left should hit the spirit in his eyes and distract him from the evil he might be planning. Another thought about spilled salt is that each grain of salt is equal to an unshed tear. If you don't want to shed so many tears, however, it is said that simply sweeping up the spilled salt and immediately tossing it into the oven will dry up all of your tears. Yet one more variation on this suggests that if the grains land on someone else at the table, the unfortunate recipient will be plagued by ill fortune. And even today, though far removed from an age where salt was equated with magic, salt is still thrown over the left shoulder to ward off bad luck.

In one of the world's most famous paintings, *The Last Supper* by Leonardo da Vinci, the negative consequences of misusing salt tell the viewer that something very dark is on the horizon. In that painting one can see that Judas has spilled the salt, foreshadowing his betrayal of Jesus Christ. Though there is no biblical evidence that salt was actually spilled at that supper, Leonardo da Vinci has incorporated the widely known superstition into his work to further dramatize the scene. Spilled salt isn't the only ill boding in this famed painting. There also happens to be an unlucky number of thirteen people at the dinner table.

Salt, too, is thought by many to grant protection against evil. By wearing a sachet of salt around your neck, evil spirits will be kept at bay. It is also well known by those in the know that salt tossed at a vampire will keep him away, too.

If you need a pinch of salt for that cake you started to bake, be careful about whom you borrow it from. Some traditions have it that lending or borrowing salt (or pepper) will destroy a friendship. If you must get that salt from your best friend, who lives next door, however, this superstition says that you should receive it as a gift rather than borrowing it and returning it later—which could lead to the end of a good relationship.

Salt has even been said to have the ability of supplying the life force itself. Another superstition involves the giving of salt to those whom you don't know very well. This superstition says that it is dangerous to give salt to a stranger and to then let him carry it away. You could end up letting the stranger carry away a portion of your life and strength with him.

Various salt superstitions can be seen among people from all over the world. In the Middle East, according to ancient Arabic folklore, it is said that when two people eat salt together a bond is formed. This long-lived tradition is still practiced today. The Arabs also have traditionally used salt to seal a bargain. The superstitions they have held about salt led them to believe that it would seal a pact. In the Arab world, if you ate a man's salt you could not harm him in any way until you left his home, and he, in turn, could not harm you either. Even to this day there is an Arabic expression, "there is salt between us," which means that we have a pact in good faith.

The Arabs are not the only ethnic group with their own interpretations of salt superstitions. Around the world, the sacredness of salt was transformed into superstitious beliefs about its powers.

"Unbaptised children are readily seized by the fairies. The best preventive is a little salt tied up in the child's dress when it is laid to sleep in the cradle," claims a warning from an old Irish book of superstitions. Old Irish and Scottish lore say that salt could protect the newborn and the dead. In both Scotland and England several handfuls of salt were placed on the chest of a corpse in order to purify the soul and to protect the dead from evil.

Hawaiians had another use for salt when dealing with the dead. An old custom warned them to sprinkle salt on themselves when they returned home from a funeral. This would ensure that evil spirits that might be hovering around the dead wouldn't follow the funeral guests into their houses.

Salt, in fact, was thought to be a great protector from evil in almost every country. Just what types of evil it protected against, however, varied from country to country. In Japan, salt was sprinkled on stages before performances to prevent evil spirits from casting a spell on the actors, thus ruining the performance. In Greece, a pinch of salt on a baby's tongue was an offering to the gods to ward off evil in the child. In medieval Europe, salt was sprinkled in rooms to ward off evil spirits that might be lurking in dark corners. And in many countries the world over, salt was scattered on the threshold of a new home to prevent evil spirits from entering.

Salt's power in Latin America included the ability to affect what happens in the future. In Mexico, it was thought that if a household ran out of salt, misfortune was lying in wait for that household in the near future. And in Germany, if a girl forgot the saltshaker in setting the table, it was an admission that she had lost her virginity. To assure that no misfortune would befall a visiting guest, the ancient Greeks greeted strangers with a pinch of salt.

Not only was salt the subject of superstitions held by the common man but it was also the center of many religious rituals. From Christians to Druids, salt has been used in religious ceremonies from the beginning of time, and it is still used today in many religions. Salt is added to the holy water in the Catholic church before the water is blessed by the priests, an ages-old tradition that stems from the days when salt was a preciously rare substance.

In primitive cultures, salt was the only substance they had that would preserve meat. Its powers were so important that they seemed magical, which made salt a highly revered commodity. When primitive peoples sacrificed animals to their gods, they placed salt on the heads of these animals first. Not only was the salt itself considered an important gift to the gods, but it also assured that the sacrificed animal would be clean and well preserved.

Worshippers of the sun god also saw salt as a great gift of the powerful god. These people saw the sun dry up seawater, leaving the remaining salt for mankind, and they considered salt to be a special gift to them from the sun god. The endless bounty of salt taken from evaporated ocean water led these people to believe that they were, indeed, well taken care of by the god of the sun.

In the Native American communities, the gods and goddesses associated with salt were some of the most important figures of worship. The Hopi believed in a very powerful god that was both the god of salt and also the god of war. He was one of the most powerful beings in their universe. The Navajos made the goddess of salt a very powerful and holy woman. And the Aztecs included their salt goddess as one of the four chief deities, who were the most important entities in their universe.

The Hebrews also made offerings of salt to Jehovah. During harvesttime, salt was offered to Jehovah in thanks for the harvest and to ensure another good harvest in the future. And the Druids used salt in their sacrifices at Stonehenge as a symbol of life-giving fruits of the earth.

The Bible itself has thirty-two references to salt—from its use in baptism to the famed story of

Lot. Lot and his family were given leave to depart from Sodom before the city was to be burned to the ground because of its corruption. They were, however, instructed not to look back during their departure. Lot's wife did not heed this advice and was turned into a pillar of salt when she did look back.

While many of the superstitions and religious rites of the past are no longer practiced or even remembered, the important place that salt once held lives on in the clichés that continue to pepper (or should I say salt) our language.

While some sayings are beginning to die out, others continue to be used by people who are unaware of their original meaning. "Pass me salt, pass me sorrow" is an old American saying based on the thought that it was bad luck to pass the salt-shaker to another person at the table. Today salt is probably the most frequently passed condiment at dinner tables across the country, and it is passed without an awareness of the negative import that it once had to people around the globe. Who knows what power salt might hold over those dinner table arguments and bad-tasting meals after all?

"He's not worth his salt" is a phrase that is still commonly used to convey the inadequacies of the person being described. This phrase is actually said to come from two different places. Some say that it originated in ancient Greece, where salt was traded for slaves. Dissatisfied slave owners meant that the slave wasn't worth the salt that they had paid for him. Others say that the phrase first came from Petronius in the *Satyricon* as opprobrium for Roman soldiers who were paid part of their salary in salt, meaning obviously that the wage earners were paid more than they were worth.

When one is "below the salt" it means that person is of the lower classes. In the old homes of the nobility, a huge saltcellar was placed on the table, dividing people according to rank. Those of the highest class sat above the salt, or near the head of the table, while the lower classes sat below the salt. Though not used as often today as some of the other salt phrases, it is still heard occasionally, despite the fact that its significance has all but disappeared.

If one is held in very high esteem, he is still referred to frequently as "the salt of the earth," and if we are to "take something with a grain of salt," we should put it in its true perspective before judging. So as you read about these superstitions, which have been revered throughout the ages, take them with a grain of salt and read on.

SALT:
THE HOUSEHOLD
ALTERNATIVE

*S*alt can solve many household problems, and it is not only a very effective alternative to regular household products, such as pesticides, cleaning agents, and beauty products, but is also an inexpensive alternative. It cleans and permeates stains such as blood that no other cleaners seem to effectively tackle. In addition, its great qualities as a preservative allow it to hold colors in such things as silk flowers and brightly colored fabrics. And precisely because salt does have a bit of a destructive quality all its own, this can be used to great advantage in preventing unwanted weed growth in nooks and crannies around the patio and on brick houses and in killing germs and odors on wooden cutting boards and around the kitchen. From natural pesticide to skin softener, the alternative uses for salt are abundant. So next time you have a household problem for which you don't know a solution, check the following handy reference guide. Chances are you'll be able to solve your problem with salt!

In the Medicine Chest

CONGESTION RELIEVER

*I*nstead of relying on over-the-counter nose sprays or wasting boxes and boxes of tissues, next time you have a congested nose try this natural, effective alternative. Saltwater rinsing helps break up local mucous congestion while it removes dust and virus particles and bacteria from your nose before your cold gets more serious. Mix $1/4$ teaspoon salt and $1/4$ teaspoon baking soda in 8 ounces warm water. Use a bulb syringe to squirt water into the nose. Hold one nostril closed while squirting the salt mixture into the other nostril. Let it drain. Repeat 2 to 3 times, then treat the other nostril. Repeat several times daily. (Don't share your syringe, and be sure to spray and wash it with hot water between dosings.)

SORE THROAT RELIEF

*G*argling with saltwater is an effective alternative to continually sucking on throat lozenges, and the temporary relief is felt immediately. Dissolve 1 teaspoon of salt in a cup of warm water. Tilt your head back and swish the liquid around at the back of your throat to moisten the sore throat and bring temporary relief. Repeat this four times daily.

CARE OF ATHLETE'S FOOT

*A*thlete's foot is caused by fungi and yeast and persists in warm, moist environments. Wearing natural cotton socks helps prevent the fungus from growing, but other measures usually must be taken to get rid of the problem. Add a handful of salt to a footbath filled with warm water and mix well. Soak foot in warm saltwater for 5 to 10 minutes at a time. This helps kill fungus and, in addition, softens the skin so that antifungal medication can penetrate better.

BABY NOSE DROPS

*F*or babies two years and under who have stuffy noses, salt can be used in a water-based solution to safely relieve congestion. To make the saline solution dissolve $1/4$ teaspoon salt in 8 ounces warm water. Insert two drops into each nostril before the infant eats or sleeps and then gently suction out the saline mixture and mucous with a bulb. It's important not to use this treatment more than six times a day.

SORE FEET RELIEF

*A*t the end of a hard day there's nothing quite like a nice warm footbath to soothe and refresh a tired pair of feet. You can create your own inexpensive spa bath for the feet by using a handful of ordinary table salt tossed into a small basin of water heated to your own level of comfort. It's much more revitalizing than a plain basin of warm water and will do wonders for your aching feet.

REHYDRATION

*F*or anyone who has ever suffered a severe or even mild bout of traveler's sickness, the loss of important fluids and electrolytes in the body is a weakening and potentially dangerous side effect of persistent diarrhea and vomiting. To prevent dehydration and maintain your electrolyte balance, it is necessary to replace the lost salt and liquid in your body by drinking a solution of water that is supplemented with ordinary salt and sugar. Combine 1 teaspoon salt and 4 teaspoons sugar in 1 quart water. Drink 1 pint of this solution per hour.

REDUCING EYE PUFFINESS

*I*f you've had a miserable episode of crying or you just couldn't get enough sleep to give your face that fresh, well-rested look, this eye-puffiness reducer will be a great relief, especially if you're on your way to a job interview or other important meeting. Mix 1 teaspoon of salt in 1 pint hot water and apply pads soaked in the solution to the puffy eye areas.

BATHING EYES

*P*eople who wear contact lenses know what a relief it is to bathe their eyes with a saline solution. The eyes immediately feel revitalized because tears themselves are really saltwater. Mix $1/2$ teaspoon salt in 1 pint of water, then place the solution in an eyedropper to bathe tired eyes.

HARD CONTACT LENS FLUID

*I*f you run out of storage fluid for your hard contact lenses, chances are you can find the ingredients right in your kitchen cupboard to tide you over until you can replace it. In a sterile container mix well ¼ teaspoon salt, ¼ teaspoon baking soda, and 1 cup sterile water until the baking soda and salt are dissolved. Pour the solution through a paper coffee filter to remove any undissolved particles and store in a sterile dropper bottle.

As a Grooming Aid

ROUGH AND CHAPPED SKIN

*O*rdinary table salt can be used to create your own customized skin relief cream. To soften rough skin in such problem spots as feet, knees, and elbows, combine $1/4$ cup salt, $1/4$ cup Epsom salts, and $1/4$ cup vegetable oil, and massage the resulting paste into the dry skin for several minutes. After the cream has refreshed your skin it can be removed by bathing or showering.

REMOVING DRY SKIN

Salt can act as an abrasive to help remove dry and flaky skin. After bathing and while still wet, give yourself a massage with dry salt on a sponge, washcloth, or pumice stone. It removes dead skin particles, exposing the more radiant skin underneath, and it also aids the circulation.

APPLYING A FACIAL

Salt can be used to create an excellent revitalizing mixture to give yourself a home facial. First wash your face and apply warm, wet towels to the skin. Then apply a mixed solution of equal parts salt and olive oil, and gently massage the face and throat with long upward and inward strokes. Remove the mixture after 5 minutes and then rinse the face and apply your favorite face lotion.

CLEANING TEETH

A nice alternative to the commercial brands of toothpaste, which generally have sugar and other ingredients to sweeten them, is a mixture of salt and baking soda. Mix 1 part salt to 2 parts baking soda after pulverizing the salt in a blender or rolling it on a kitchen board with a tumbler before mixing. It whitens the helps remove plaque, and is healthy for the gums.

MOUTHWASH

A homemade natural mouthwash can be made from a few simple ingredients right out of your kitchen cabinet. Place 1 teaspoon salt and 1 teaspoon baking soda in $1/2$ cup water and rinse or gargle. It is a mouthwash that will sweeten the breath. For those who like a minty taste, try adding a few drops of peppermint extract to the solution. This solution is particularly good for those who may have had recent dental work or any other injury of the mouth or gums.

The use of table salt accounts for only approximately 5 percent of the total usage of salt.

PREVENT YOUR PANTYHOSE
FROM RUNNING

*T*here's nothing more annoying than buying a brand-new pair of pantyhose and running them as you put them on for the first time. To help prevent runs altogether, wash new pantyhose and allow to drip dry. Then mix 2 cups salt with 1 gallon water and immerse the pantyhose. Soak for 3 hours, rinse in cold water, and drip dry.

DRY SKIN

*S*alt can be used to successfully soothe dry skin. You can simply add about 1/2 cup per tubful of warm water to create a bath that is mildly salty. This also will help you with any aches or pains that you may be experiencing. To finish off your treatment, apply a moisturizing cream or lotion to rehydrate your body.

ITCHY SKIN

*F*or skin that is chapped or itchy for any number of reasons (poison ivy, insect bites, food allergy rashes, or postsunburn skin peeling), bathing in saltwater is soothing. Just add $^1/_2$ to 1 cup salt to a bath of warm water. After bathing, smooth on aloe vera gel or any other skin refreshers or creams for immediate, soothing relief.

OILY SKIN

S alt can be used to restore a healthy balance to your skin and to exfoliate oily skin the natural way, without using products that are filled with artificial chemicals. All you have to do to start the treatment is to open your pores up with a hot, moist towel applied to the face for about 5 minutes. Then fill a small spray bottle with tepid water and 1 teaspoon salt, and spray the solution on your face. Afterward, blot your face dry with a clean towel. This treatment leaves your skin feeling healthy and refreshed without being too dry or too oily.

People have to eat more salt in very hot climates, where much salt is lost in perspiration. Doctors often advise people who are going for a long stay in a hot country to take salt tablets with them.

In the Bathroom

BATHROOM DRAIN CLEANER

*T*o help dissolve scum and hair in sluggish bathroom sink and tub drains, pour a mixture of 1 cup salt, 1 cup baking soda, and $1/2$ cup white vinegar into the drain. Then let stand for 15 minutes and flush with 2 quarts boiling water followed by flushing hot tap water down the drain for 1 minute. You can repeat this process if necessary.

PORCELAIN STAIN REMOVER

*T*hose nice colored bathroom porcelain sinks and tubs can become stained with water marks and other substances that are hard to remove without scratching the finish. This gentle scouring powder will help remove those stains without scratching the surfaces. Mix 1 cup salt with 1 cup baking soda and keep in a sealed container for continued use. Use the mixture as you would any scouring powder.

YELLOWED TUB

*A*fter a few years even the cleanest of house-keepers may find that the tub or sink has a troublesome yellowish brown color building up on the surface from rust or other minerals in the water. To remove this discoloration from a yellowed bathtub or sink, rub the tub or sink with a solution of equal parts salt and turpentine. Be sure to wear rubber gloves and to open the bathroom or kitchen window and follow up by rinsing thoroughly after the stains are gone.

In the Cleaning Closet

GENTLE SCOURING POWDER

*T*his gentle scouring powder will work as well as most commercial brands and is among the most gentle cleaners for stains in colored porcelain sinks and on easily scratchable kitchen countertops. Add 1 cup salt to 1 cup baking soda and blend well. Store in a covered container and keep on hand with your other cleaning supplies.

GREASE SPOTS ON RUGS

*I*f you have a problem with messy kids or Sunday couch potatoes who are prone to knocking over greasy food on the rug, table salt can be an effective de-greaser that can get your rug back to normal. The cleaning solution can be made by mixing 1 part salt to 4 parts rubbing alcohol. Take the mixture and rub it hard over the spot, but be careful to rub in the direction of the natural nap of the rug while cleaning the stain so as to avoid damaging the nap.

SPILLED KETCHUP
ON NYLON CARPETING

*K*etchup or other tomato sauces can be really stubborn stains to remove from ordinary carpeting. Salt can help prevent the stain from permanently seeping into the rug. As soon as possible after the tomato sauce is spilled, sprinkle carpeting with enough salt to soak up the stain. Remove the excess salt and repeat as many times as necessary until the stain is removed. Finish by vacuuming up the messy mixture and use a dampened sponge to remove any residual stain that is left on the carpet.

SPILLED RED WINE

*A*mong the worst of stains to remove is red wine. But salt can really do the trick and help prevent your carpet from forever reminding you of the wine that was served at your last dinner party. After the red wine is spilled on the carpet, dilute it with white wine, then clean the spot with cold water and cover with table salt. Wait 10 minutes and vacuum up the salt and wine mixture.

COPPER

*T*he original shiny luster can be restored to copper by removing the green tarnish that occurs when copper oxidizes. To make the cleaning solution, combine 1 tablespoon salt, 1 tablespoon flour, and 1 tablespoon vinegar, then rub over the surface of the copper and follow by washing in hot soapy water. Rinse with water and dry with a soft cloth before buffing until the original shine is restored.

Another equally effective way to use salt to clean your copper items is to cut a lemon in half, dip it in salt, and rub it over the surface of the copper. Wash the surface with soapy water and then rinse, dry, and buff.

BRASS

*Y*our favorite brass candleholders, fireplace implements, doorknobs, or handrails can be restored to their original brilliance by combining 1 tablespoon salt, 1 tablespoon flour, and 1 tablespoon vinegar. Then apply the paste with a soft cloth and rub until all of the tarnish has been removed. Follow by washing in warm soapy water and rinsing and buffing

Another equally effective way to use salt to clean your brass items is to dip a cut lemon in salt and rub it on the brass. Follow by washing in warm soapy water, rinse with normal water, and buff it dry to bring up the shine.

WICKER

*T*he life of wicker patio furniture, baskets, or any other wicker items can be extended by using salt. To prevent yellowing, scrub wicker furniture with a stiff brush moistened with warm salt-water and allow to dry in the sun.

YELLOWED IVORY

*O*ld piano keys or anything else that is made from ivory can be cleaned by using salt. Cut a lemon in half, dip it in salt, and rub over the ivory surface. Let it dry, wipe the object with a cloth, and buff it dry for a bright finish.

BURNED COOKWARE

*S*alt acts as an effective abrasive for burns on your cookware, and because it is natural, you don't have to worry about residual chemical cleaners on the surfaces of cookware. Wet the burned spot, sprinkle with salt, let stand for 10 minutes, and scrub well.

COFFEE- OR TEA-STAINED CUPS

*W*hile many restaurants use bleach to remove the stains left by coffee and tea, a much healthier alternative can be found by using salt. Simply scrub these stubborn stains with salt sprinkled on a sponge, or if you need a stronger cleaner, try a mixture of equal parts salt and white vinegar to remove these ugly brown stains from your light or brightly colored coffee mugs and teacups.

RINGS ON FURNITURE LEFT BY CUPS OR GLASSES

When your guests have neglected the coasters you so prominently displayed and you find that wet glasses have left unsightly stains on your nice wood tabletops, you can remove the stains with nothing more than salt. Use a pinch of table salt and a drop of water and then apply to the stain ring with the end of a cloth or sponge and scrub until the stain disappears. Follow with your regular furniture polish to restore the shine to the wood.

STAINS FROM LIQUID INK

A leaky pen in a shirt or pants pocket can ruin a good piece of clothing. If the ink is still wet, pour salt on the stain and gently dab at the stain, being careful not to spread it around the area that surrounds the stain. Brush it off after a few minutes; repeat if necessary.

STAINS ON VASES

*F*lower vases are prone to ugly brown stains from flowers left too long in unchanged water. Plain salt acts as a perfect scouring agent to get rid of these stains. To remove water rings, rub with salt. If the vase is narrow and you can't reach inside, fill the vase with a strong saltwater solution and shake until clean. Follow by washing as usual.

SCOURING CUTTING BOARDS, POTS, AND PANS

*K*itchen implements often need a good cleaning, and yet it can be a source of concern to use chemical products on the surfaces that we eat off of and prepare food in. Damp salt is a good scouring agent for kitchen utensils and is safer than chemical cleaning agents. Simply use the damp salt on a sponge or other cleaning implement and scour as usual.

GLASS COFFEEPOT CARAFES

*I*f you've ever worked in a restaurant that serves lots of coffee, you're bound to know this handy trick to keep the pots looking fresh and new. This old method of cleaning has been and continues to be used by waiters and waitresses everywhere. All you have to do is put into a coffeepot 2 tablespoons salt, enough ice to cover the bottom, and the juice of 1 lemon, quartered, as well as the cut lemon pieces themselves, and swirl the contents in a circular motion until the coffee stains lift from the glass surface. The stains and burned-on coffee residue lift right off. When finished just empty out the contents of the carafe and clean as usual with dishwashing liquid and water.

OVEN SPILLS

*S*alt is a very good alternative to the awful-smelling and chemically toxic oven cleaners that are typically used. When something cooking in the oven bubbles over, quickly sprinkle the stain with salt to prevent the spill from adhering to the surface, and then the stain will be easily wiped away with a paper towel.

GREASY PANS

*T*he greasiest iron pan will wash more easily if you put a little salt in it and follow up by wiping the surface with paper towels and cleaning as usual.

CLEANING STOVE BURNERS

*S*alt will clean stove burners as well as the oven inside. Sprinkle spills while the stove burners are still hot; when dry, remove the salted spots with a stiff brush or cloth. Salt also helps remove the unwanted odors from any spilled-over food on the stove or in the oven.

CLEANING REFRIGERATORS

*S*alt and soda water will clean and freshen the inside of your refrigerator. The great thing about using this mixture is that it is naturally nonabrasive and is safe for using on the easily scratchable surfaces that coat the insides of refrigerators. Since it is also natural, it will spare you from contaminating the food inside with chemical odors and fumes.

TARNISHED SILVERWARE

*T*he simple act of rubbing the tarnish with salt before washing as usual helps to remove the silverware tarnish.

EXTEND BROOM AND BRUSH LIFE

*N*ew brooms and cleaning brushes will wear longer if soaked in hot saltwater before they are first used. Add 1 cup salt to a bucket of steaming water and soak your new brooms and brushes in the mixture. Use this liquid to freshen your old sponges after you've finished.

RESTORING SPONGES

*W*hether it's the one on the kitchen sink or the one on your mop, sponges can get very dirty before the sponge itself is ready to be changed. Give old sponges and mop heads new life by soaking them in saltwater after they've been washed. Use about 1/4 cup salt per quart of water to make the soaking solution.

CREATE A HOMEMADE
AIR FRESHENER

*Y*ou can make your own natural and inexpensive air freshener with table salt and oranges or lemons. Cut an orange or lemon in half, remove the pulp, and fill the peel with salt. It provides a pleasant, aromatic scent.

CLEANING FISH TANKS

*T*he glass surface of home aquariums can become cloudy and discolored. Try using this salt solution to clean the surface of the tank. To remove the hard water deposits, rub the inside of the fish tank with salt sprinkled on a damp sponge or cloth, then rinse well before returning the fish to the tank. Use only plain, not iodized, salt.

REMOVING SOOT

*W*hile we think of chimney sweeps as a thing of the past, the truth is that soot buildup in a chimney can cause dangerous fires. Occasionally throw a handful of salt on the flames in your fireplace to help loosen soot from the chimney. The salt will also make a beautiful, bright yellow flame.

DEODORIZING SHOES

*E*veryone who wears summer canvas shoes with bare feet knows that the shoes can become moist and odor-filled from sweaty feet. Occasionally sprinkling a little salt in canvas shoes will take up the moisture and help remove odors.

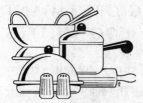

In the Kitchen

PREVENTING FOOD
FROM STICKING

*R*ub a pancake griddle with a small bag of salt to prevent sticking and smoking. Sprinkle a little salt in the skillet before frying fish to prevent the fish from sticking. Sprinkle salt on washed skillets, waffle iron plates, or griddles, then heat in a warm oven and dust off salt; when they are next used, foods will not stick.

PREVENT CHEESE
FROM MOLDING

*S*alt can be used successfully to extend the life of cheese and to protect it from molding in your refrigerator. Take your cheese and wrap it in a cloth dampened with saltwater before refrigerating.

WHIPPING CREAM AND BEATING EGG WHITES

*I*f you add a pinch of salt, cream will whip better than normal. If you add a pinch of salt before beginning to beat egg whites, they will also beat faster and higher and will firm up better.

KEEPING MILK FRESH

*S*alt can help milk and cream stay fresher longer and prevent these dairy products from spoiling. Add a pinch of salt to milk and cream to extend the shelf life of these products in your refrigerator.

SETTING GELATIN

*I*f you got started a little too late to have that gelatin salad chilled and set before the guests arrive, try this trick to speed things up a bit. To set gelatin salads and desserts quickly, place them over ice that has been sprinkled with salt.

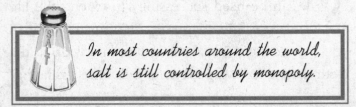

In most countries around the world, salt is still controlled by monopoly.

REMOVING ONION ODORS
FROM HANDS

*T*he smell of onions and garlic can really stay on your hands long after you've done the chopping. Rub your fingers with salt moistened with vinegar and you'll find that this mixture will act as a natural deodorizer for your hands in the kitchen.

DEODORIZING CONTAINERS

*S*alt can deodorize thermos bottles and jugs, decanters, and closed containers. Fill the container with warm water and add a teaspoon or so of salt, depending on the size of the container. Let stand for an hour or so, even overnight if the container smells very sour, then wash with soap and warm water as usual.

IMPROVING COFFEE

*A*n old European trick for improving the flavor of coffee is to add a pinch of salt. Simply put a pinch of salt in the filter with the coffee before brewing. It will enhance the flavor. You can also remove the bitterness of overheated coffee by adding a pinch of salt to your cup.

IMPROVING POULTRY

*S*alt can be used to enhance the flavor of poultry even before it is cooked. To improve the flavor of all types of poultry, rub the fowl inside and out with salt before roasting.

REMOVING PINFEATHERS

*T*o remove the pinfeathers easily from a chicken, goose, or duck, rub the skin with salt first and then pluck away.

PEELING EGGS

*Y*ou'll find that boiled eggs will peel much more easily if you add a little salt. Simply add a pinch or two of salt to the boiling water before putting the eggs in it.

POACHING EGGS

*T*he whites of poached eggs will stay together much more easily with the addition of a little salt. Add salt to boiling water before dropping the eggs into it to help set the egg whites.

TESTING EGG FRESHNESS

*I*f you have eggs that you think might have been in the refrigerator for too long, you can use salt to test an egg's freshness. Place the questionable egg in a cup of water to which 2 teaspoons salt have been added. A fresh egg will sink; a questionable egg will float.

PREVENTING BROWNING

*I*t's shocking just how fast some fruits and vegetables brown after they've been cut. Apples, pears, and potatoes dropped in cold, lightly salted water as they are peeled will retain their just-cut color longer.

SHELLING PECANS

*Y*ou'll find that the outer portion of pecans can be much more easily removed by using salt. Just soak the pecans in saltwater for several hours before shelling, and this will make the nut meats easier to remove.

The early Chinese used coins made of salt for currency.

WASHING SPINACH

*T*he sand on spinach or other freshly picked garden greens can be more easily removed with salt. If greens are washed in salted water, repeated cleanings will not be necessary.

PREVENTING SUGARING

*Y*our frosted deserts, too, can be improved by a bit of salt. A good trick to keeping frosted desserts from becoming old-looking is to add a little salt to cake icings. This will prevent them from sugaring.

CRISPING SALADS

*W*hen you entertain guests, it might ease your burden a little to know that by salting the salads early, they will stay fresh longer, so you can prepare the salads in advance of your dinner party. If you add a pinch of salt, the salted salads will also have improved textures. Simply salt salads to taste immediately before serving to prevent premature wilting of lettuces and other greens.

IMPROVING BOILED POTATOES

*S*alt can really improve the texture of freshly boiled potatoes. Simply coat the potatoes with salt after draining, then return them to the pan and shake them back and forth quickly to get rid of the excess water.

KEEP GARLIC FROM STICKING TO THE MINCING KNIFE

*W*hen mincing garlic, sprinkle salt on the cutting board where you will be mincing the garlic and also sprinkle salt on the clove of garlic. The salt acts as an abrasive, preventing the knife from sticking to the garlic.

REMOVE ODORS FROM GARBAGE DISPOSALS

*T*he garbage disposal in your kitchen sink can benefit from an extra salt cleaning from time to time. Salt can be used to clean and freshen your garbage disposal quickly and easily. Just pour $\frac{1}{2}$ cup salt directly into the garbage disposal. Then run water and activate the disposal as usual.

AS A STOVETOP
FIRE EXTINGUISHER

*I*f there is a fire on top of the stove, you should first turn off the burner, leave the pan where it is, and smother the flames with the lid. In most cases this alone will put out the fire. If this does not immediately work, however, douse the fire with handfuls of salt.

REMOVE ODORS FROM YOUR
WOODEN CUTTING BOARD

*S*alt works well to remove stubborn odors from wooden chopping boards, such as those that remain after garlic and onions have been chopped. Pour a generous amount of salt onto your cutting board. Rub lightly with a damp cloth. Wash in warm, sudsy water, and your wooden chopping board will be clean and fresh and ready for the next meal.

CLEAN UP SPILLED EGGS

*T*here's nothing worse to clean up than an egg that has broken onto the kitchen floor or countertop. Salt can be used to make this slippery mess much easier to clean. Pour salt over the top of the spill to cover the eggs. Then wipe the eggs up with a paper towel and follow up by cleaning the surface as usual.

In the Laundry

FIX STICKING IRON

*S*ticky spots on an iron can really ruin a clean white shirt or other fabric. Salt can be used to easily remove the tarlike substance from the surface of your household iron. Sprinkle a little salt on a piece of paper and run the hot iron over it to remove the rough, sticky spots. Repeat, if necessary, until the troublesome substance had been completely removed.

FRESHEN YOUR LAUNDRY AND PREVENT IRON FROM STICKING

*Y*ou'll be surprised by the improvements in ironing that a little bit of salt will make. A dash of salt in laundry starch keeps the iron from sticking and gives linens and fine cottons a glossy, brand-new finish.

REMOVE MILDEW STAINS

*B*efore you dispose of that mildewy old garment that has been sitting in your closet or attic just a bit too long, first try using a little bit of salt and lemon to freshen it. Moisten stained spots with a mixture of lemon juice and salt, then spread the item in the sun for bleaching; finally, rinse and dry. Follow up by laundering as usual.

REMOVE BLOODSTAINS

*B*loodstains can be among the toughest stains to remove from clothing and fabrics. Soak the stained clothing or cloth in cold saltwater, then launder in warm, soapy water, and boil after the wash.

(Use only on cotton, linen, or other natural fibers that can take high heat.)

BRIGHTEN YELLOWED COTTONS OR LINENS

Cotton and linen items can appear old well before their time, but salt can be used to remove the yellow cast and brighten these fabrics. Boil the yellowed items for 1 hour in a solution of water and equal parts salt and baking soda, using ½ cup each per gallon of water used.

REMOVING PERSPIRATION STAINS

Yellowed perspiration stains can really ruin otherwise usable T-shirts and dress shirts. Salt can be used to give these stained items a new life. Add 4 tablespoons salt to 1 quart hot water, and sponge the fabric with the solution until stains disappear.

> *The Bible has thirty-two references to salt, chiefly in connection with sacrifices and covenants.*

BRIGHTENING COLORS

*W*ash colored curtains or washable fiber rugs in a saltwater solution to brighten the colors. Brighten faded rugs and carpets by rubbing them briskly with a cloth that has been dipped in a strong saltwater solution and wrung out.

REMOVE WINE STAINS FROM COTTON FABRIC

*A*nybody who has ever tried to remove a wine or grape juice stain from an item of cotton clothing knows that it is usually a lost cause. Salt can be of great use in this situation. Immediately pour salt on the fabric to soak up the stain and then immerse the fabric in cold water for half an hour. Follow this up by laundering the item as usual.

SOFTEN NEW JEANS

*T*he uncomfortable stiffness of a pair of new denim jeans can be easily remedied by adding $1/2$ cup salt to the water in your automatic washer along with detergent. Your jeans will be soft and supple from the first time that you wear them.

SETTLING SUDS

*I*f a washing machine bubbles over from too many suds, sprinkle salt on the suds to reduce them. You can do the same for a tub of dishwater in which the bubbles have gotten out of control or a bubble bath that is overflowing onto your bathroom floor. Adding salt is an old college trick to settle the foam in a glass of beer that has been poured too quickly.

RUST STAINS ON
WASHABLE GARMENTS

*R*ust stains are one of the trickiest stains to remove with commercial cleaners, but this simple salt solution defies the idea that they are impossible to remove. Rub a paste of equal parts salt and vinegar into the stain; let stand for 30 minutes, then launder as usual.

Salt is used in over 14,000 industrial processes and is essential in the manufacture of nearly every chemical product on the market.

In the Garage

AUTO FLOOR CLEANERS

*I*t's easy to track greasy stains into your car, especially if you've had leaky oil in your garage. With a mixture of salt and baking soda, you can freshen your car carpet and upholstery and get rid of the unsightly stains. Absorb the greasy stains with a mixture that is equal parts salt and baking soda. Sprinkle the powder on the stain, brush lightly, leave for a few hours, then vacuum.

REMOVE RUST FROM BICYCLE HANDLEBARS AND TIRE RIMS

*W*e all know that salt can cause metal to rust, but this trick actually comes in handy for removing rust from the metal parts of bicycles, like handlebars and tire rims. Make a paste using 6 table-spoons salt and 2 tablespoons lemon juice. Apply paste to rusted area with a dry cloth and rub. Rinse thoroughly and dry.

TO REMOVE THE RUST FROM HOUSEHOLD TOOLS

*T*ools left in a damp garage for long periods between use have a tendency to get rusty and useless. You can give these tools a new life by making a paste using 2 tablespoons salt and 1 tablespoon lemon juice. Apply the paste to rusted areas with a dry cloth and rub. Rinse thoroughly and dry.

PREVENT SNOW AND ICE FROM COLLECTING ON CAR WINDOWS

*I*f you live in a cold climate, you know how frustrating it can be to have to scrape the snow and ice off of your car windows every morning. You can prevent the snow and ice from collecting, however, by filling a small cloth bag with salt, dampening the bag, and rubbing it over the car windows.

In the Yard

PREVENTING CABBAGE WORMS

*A*ny backyard gardener knows that cabbage worms seem to appear out of nowhere to infest cabbage leaves. Instead of using chemical pesticides, however, you can try this natural way to get rid of the annoying pest. Lightly dust leaves with a powdered mixture of $1/2$ cup salt and 1 cup flour. Apply to plants while they are wet with dew.

KILL SLUGS

*S*prinkle salt on slugs to kill them. Stage an evening raid in the garden with a saltshaker in hand. Sprinkle each slug once, then again in 5 minutes. You'll find that your vegetables will be quickly saved from these unsightly garden pests.

PREVENT GRASS FROM GROWING BETWEEN PATIO BRICKS

A lovely brick patio can look very disheveled once grass and weeds begin to take root in between the bricks. To discourage the grass and weeds from growing between bricks on a patio or bricks on a wall, sprinkle salt in the crevices.

TO KILL POISON IVY

S alt can be used as a nontoxic herbicide to kill poison ivy from the overgrown areas of your lawn or garden. Mix 3 pounds salt with 1 gallon soapy water and apply to leaves and stems with a sprayer.

RELIEVING BEESTINGS

T he pain and swelling caused by beestings can be alleviated by using salt. If stung by a bee, immediately wet the afflicted area and cover with salt. The pain and swelling should then subside.

TREATING MOSQUITO AND CHIGGER BITES

*Y*ou can alleviate the itching and irritation of these insect bites by soaking the afflicted areas in saltwater, then applying a mixture of lard or vegetable shortening and salt.

TREATING POISON IVY

*I*f you've found yourself coming into contact with this nasty plant, try soaking the areas exposed in hot saltwater, which will quickly relieve the irritation caused by poison ivy.

An ancient belief held that good spirits stood behind a person's right shoulder and bad spirits stood behind his left. Thus the maxim that you should toss a pinch of salt over your left shoulder was coined because it was believed that such salt would hit the bad spirit in the eye, distracting him from his evil deeds.

At the Shore

REMOVE LEECHES

*F*or those lakeside vacations where leeches attach themselves to swimmers, here is a very convenient remedy to an alarming situation. Shaking salt directly onto the leeches that have attached themselves will cause them to shrivel up and fall off.

REMOVE JELLYFISH

A beach vacation can really be ruined by the sting of a jellyfish. A mixture of equal parts vinegar and saltwater when poured over the site of a jellyfish sting will deactivate the tentacles, which should then be scraped off with a towel or with sand held by a towel—not the hand. Pull off—do not rub—the tentacles. The tentacles will continue to discharge their stinging cells as long as they remain on the skin.

In the Playroom

SUBSTITUTE FOR CLAY

*Y*our kids will enjoy making this fun, puttylike substance that will eventually harden to preserve their masterpieces for later viewing and enjoyment. Combine 1 cup salt, $^1/_2$ cup cornstarch, and $^3/_4$ cup cold water. Mix the ingredients together in a double boiler and heat, stirring constantly for 2 to 3 minutes until thick. Remove the mixture from the heat, allow to cool, and then knead for several minutes until an even consistency is attained. It is now ready for use. This is an excellent substitute for clay because it doesn't shrink when drying, will harden to the consistency of stone, and doesn't powder like clay.

SUBSTITUTE FOR PLAY-DOH

A homemade, inexpensive, nontoxic alternative to Play-Doh can be easily made from items that you already have in your kitchen cupboard. Combine $1/2$ cup salt, 1 cup flour, 2 tablespoons vegetable oil, and $1/2$ cup water. If you wish to add a little food coloring, it will give the mixture a custom-colored appearance that your kids are bound to enjoy. Store the mixture in an airtight container or a plastic bag and let your kids make all of their fantastic figures again and again with this fun homemade material.

NOISY, SALT-FILLED BALLOONS

A dd a little life to your children's birthday parties with a small amount of salt and common balloons. Just put about a teaspoon of salt into balloons before blowing them up to give them a shaking sound like circus balloons. Little children and babies will enjoy playing with and listening to them.

NOTE: Broken balloons can be a serious choking hazard for young children and babies.

COLORED SALT PAINTINGS AND SCULPTURES

*Y*ou can use salt to create a colorful home craft material to make beautiful bottled salt sculptures or salt paintings. Separate desired portions of salt into various jars. Using a sharp knife, scrape the edge of a piece of colored chalk, allowing the colored dust to fall into a jar of salt. Firmly shake the jar of salt and colored dust to produce colored salt. Once you have the desired colors, you can either combine them in layers in a jar to create a pretty sand sculpture or you can sprinkle it on paper treated with glue, as you would use glitter to create a unique painting.

COLORED SALT GLITTER

*M*aking your own homemade glitter with salt allows you to create your own favorite colors for enhancing homemade cards and art projects. Add 1 tablespoon liquid watercolor to $1/4$ cup salt. Spread out on paper towels and microwave for 2 minutes. Using fingers, break up any dried clumps.

MUMMIES

*J*ust like the ancient Egyptians, you can make your own mummies using the following recipe.

> *¹/₄ cup salt*
> *¹/₂ cup baking soda*
> *¹/₂ cup washing soda (Washing soda is simply sodium carbonate and can be found in the laundry products section of most supermarkets.)*
> *1 apple*

Mix the salt, baking soda, and washing soda in a small container. Cut the apple into 4 equal pieces. Completely bury one of the apple quarters in the mixture and eat the other three. Every 2 days, check that the apple is drying out and then rebury it. After 10 days, you'll have a mummified piece of apple. The apple, like a mummy, will last for a long time.

SALT DOUGH PLAQUES

*M*ake your own homemade plaques with this fun and easy recipe. You can also make homemade frames for your children's artwork or family photographs with the same recipe.

1¹/₃ cups salt
1¹/₃ cups flour
1 tablespoon oil
Water
Baking tray and drawing paper
Paper clips
Paints
Paintbrushes
Varnish

1. Preheat the oven to 350 degrees.

2. Mix the salt, flour, and oil together. Add water a little at a time until you have a big ball of dough.

3. Knead the dough on a floured surface until very smooth and elastic. If too dry, add water; if too moist, put more flour on the surface.

4. Draw the shape of your plague on drawing paper. Sprinkle the paper with flour and then press a lump of dough on the paper to fill the drawn shape. Remove the dough from the paper and place on a lightly greased baking tray.

5. Roll out some dough shapes, or make letters with thick dough sausages and press them carefully onto your plaque. Push a paper clip into the top so you can hang it when it's finished.

6. Put the baking tray into the oven and bake in the middle of the oven until hard—about $1^1/_2$ hours.

7. When finished and cool, you can paint it with watercolor, poster, or gouache paints. It's best to let one color dry before you start on the next.

8. When the paint has dried, varnish your plaque. Varnish the front, let dry, then do the back. It is best to use three coats of varnish.

Around the House

TO BRIGHTEN SILK FLOWERS

To preserve the brightness of silk flowers, put them in a large paper bag and pour in 2 cups iodized salt. Close the bag and shake well. After a few minutes remove the flowers and shake off the excess salt.

TO PREVENT PIPES
FROM FREEZING

*C*old winter temperatures can cause the water in plumbing to freeze and make pipes burst, resulting in an expensive bill from the plumber, but salt can help to prevent your pipes from running into trouble during the colder months of the year. Sprinkle salt down waste pipes to keep them from freezing in very cold weather or to thaw frozen pipes.

TO PATCH NAIL HOLES AND
CRACKS IN PLASTERBOARD AND
WALLBOARD

*I*f you've grown tired of the paintings and other wall hangings in your apartment or home and want to change things around, you'll find that some surprisingly unsightly holes will be evident after you've taken out the nails and picture hooks from behind the paintings or prints. You can use this handy salt mixture to fill in the holes and restore your walls to their original condition. Mix 2 tablespoons salt, 2 tablespoons cornstarch, and about 4 to 5 teaspoons water to make a thick, pliable paste.

Fill the hole and let dry. Lightly sand or go over the raised spot with a dampened sponge to smooth it out, then paint.

TO QUICKLY CHILL CHAMPAGNE OR WINE

*I*f you've forgotten to put the wine or champagne in the refrigerator and there's enough time before your party is to begin, you can use salt and ice to quickly chill it and get it ready to serve. Place the bottle in an ice bucket or other tall plastic container. Add a layer of ice on the bottom and sprinkle it with a few tablespoons of salt. Continue to layer salt and ice until it reaches the neck of the bottle. Then add enough water to bring it up to the level of the ice. After 10 to 12 minutes, open and serve and you'll be pouring refreshingly cool beverages to your guests.

TO PREVENT DRINKS FROM STICKING TO NAPKINS AND COASTERS

*T*he moisture from drinking glasses can cause them to carry the napkins and coasters with them when you lift the glass for a sip. To prevent this, sprinkle salt on the napkins and cardboard coasters on which you set cold drinks.

TO MAKE CANDLES DRIP-PROOF

*I*f you want to save some money on candles by buying ones that are cheaper, yet prone to dripping, you can use this saltwater solution to prevent the candle wax from spilling all over the candleholders. Soak new candles in a strong salt solution for a few hours, then dry them well. When the candles are burning they will not drip.

TO INVIGORATE GOLDFISH

*O*ccasionally add 1 teaspoon salt to a quart of freshwater at room temperature and put your goldfish in for about 15 minutes. Then return them to their tank. The salt swim makes them healthier and livelier.

TO KEEP CUT FLOWERS FRESH

*W*hen you get your fresh flowers home, you should first cut off the bottoms of the stems so the flowers can easily absorb the water they are placed in. A dash of salt added to the water in a flower vase will then keep the cut flowers fresh longer.

TO HOLD ARTIFICIAL FLOWERS

*A*rtificial flowers can be gathered together in a fixed position to make an artistic arrangement by pouring salt into a decorative container, then adding a little cold water and afterward arranging the flowers. The salt will solidify as it dries and hold the flowers in place.

TO KEEP WINDOWS FROST FREE

*I*f you live in a cold climate, you know how common it is to wake up and not be able to see out your windows which have become covered with frost. To remedy the situation rub the inside of windows with a sponge dipped in a saltwater solution and rub dry; the windows will not frost up in subfreezing weather.

TO DRIVE AWAY ANTS

*I*n the hot and sticky days of summer, small ants seem to appear from nowhere to invade your house. To keep the ants away spread a thin line of salt across any entry where ants seem to be entering your house. Ants will not cross a line of salt.

SALT'S
MANY UNEXPECTED
EVERYDAY USES

When we think of salt's most common usage, the ever-present saltshaker on every American's table is the first image that comes to mind. The really surprising thing, however, is that the table usage of salt accounts for only approximately 5 percent of the total usage of salt. The other 95 percent, remarkably, is used in thousands of other ways in many unexpected places. Without salt, it is safe to say our modern manner of living would be completely different from what we now know.

America's biggest consumer of salt is the chemical industry. The combination of one atom of sodium and one atom of chlorine makes up the crucial substance that is responsible for so many different uses. In fact, 66 percent of all the salt produced is used in the chemical industry, and of 150 of the most important chemicals in current use in the United States, salt plays a major role in the production of a total of 104 of them. A few of these that you may have heard of are: hydrochloric acid, sodium bicarbonate, sodium nitrate, sodium sulfate, sodium carbonate, sodium sulfate, chlorine, caustic soda, and sodium.

The paper on which I am writing was bleached with salt, the wooden desk that lies under the paper was cured with salt, and the glass in the window next to the desk was also made with salt. The fabric in my trousers was cleansed in a salt solution, the threads that hold them together were also strengthened by salt, and the dye that produced its color was made permanent by salt. Even the leather that makes up my shoes was preserved by a salt solution.

Salt is used in the manufacturing process of some typical household items like soap, color televisions, paint, wallpaper, scouring powder, cheese, butter, plastic combs, and toothbrushes. Industrial materials like brass, bronze, steel, gold, silver, and glass also utilize salt in their production. Insecticides, herbicides, and countless other everyday chemicals could not be made without it. And in our kitchen cabinets and refrigerators, we can find many foods that are made with salt. It is used to make ice cream, cure hams, bacon, and salmon, canned goods, and the many different pickles that we enjoy so much. It also is important in the process that makes the naturally bitter taste of chocolate mild and sweet.

Our wastewater is purified and made safe with salt, and hard water in our homes is made soft with the addition of salt. Crude oil is refined with salt to make gasoline, and nuclear reactors, as well as other refrigerated systems, are cooled with the addition of salt.

Second to the chemical industry in consumption and usage of salt is the highway industry. Salt is used by those who build roads, and in the colder regions of the country, it is crucial in keeping them free of dangerous ice in the winter months. Only one pound of salt is required to melt forty-six pounds of ice at thirty degrees Fahrenheit. When making roads, salt is crucial to the manufacture of the roadbed upon which the concrete or asphalt is then placed. Highway construction crews mix salt with the clay, sand, gravel, and stone before putting down the top surface. This usage keeps the diverse mixture together by allowing it to retain moisture that it would otherwise lose. If this moisture weren't there, the underlying roadbed would crumble, resulting in the ultimate collapse of the concrete or asphalt above it.

It's safe to say that we are always within arm's reach of something that could not have been made without salt. We are extremely fortunate that today salt is in ready abundance all over the globe and that the oceans that cover our planet are filled with saltwater, because without this life-giving substance, all the living creatures in our world would have an entirely different existence.

SALTY FAVORITES: RECIPES FOR SALT DISHES

*S*alt is used in almost all recipes for taste. It enhances the taste of food for the human palate and is thus a crucial addition to almost everything. The taste for salt alone has led to an entire industry of salt-heavy foods, from potato chips to french fries, and has thus become equated with bad eating habits. But a nice salty snack in Turkey is a fresh cucumber, peeled on the spot by one of the many street vendors and given a healthy dosing of salt. Not only does the salt add a wonderful flavor to the cucumber but it also replenishes the body with a much-needed nutrient that is lost so quickly under the hot sun of Turkey. Another wonderful salty snack is a fresh tomato, straight out of the garden, sliced into nice clean wedges all sprinkled with salt.

There are essentially three types of food salt: table salt, sea salt, and kosher salt. While chemically they are all essentially the same, coming either from the sea or from salt mines, where huge deposits of salt are left from dried seas, many people feel strongly about which type of salt they use in their kitchen. Ask any chef what types of salt he uses and he will have very definite answers.

Table salt is made by driving water into a salt deposit and evaporating the brine that is formed, leaving dried cubelike crystals that are very fine. It is treated with additives to keep it flowing in all types of weather, even very humid air. It is also the only salt available with iodine, which prevents hyperthyroidism, or goiter.

Kosher salt is made in much the same way as table salt, except that it is raked continuously during the evaporation process, giving it a flakier texture. Because the grains are airier than those of table salt, they taste less salty when measured precisely. Table salt is much denser than kosher salt.

Sea salt, which comes in fine or coarse crystals, is made from seawater that has been evaporated, leaving just salt crystals. It is often preferred by health-conscious consumers because it contains additional trace minerals. But experts say that real sea salt with all of the minerals left in would be too bitter to eat. Most sea salt has been filtered so that it is nearly the same as pure table salt.

While most people use table salt for baking

because of its more precise ability to be measured, kosher salt and sea salt are widely used for cooking and sprinkling on food as well.

Salt Water Taffy

> 2 cups sugar
> 1 cup light corn syrup
> 1 cup water
> 1½ teaspoons salt
> 2 tablespoons margarine or butter
> ¼ teaspoon peppermint extract, cinnamon flavoring, or other flavoring extract of choice (optional)
> Few drops of food coloring (optional)

1. Butter the sides of a heavy 2-quart saucepan. In the saucepan combine the sugar, corn syrup, water, and salt. Cook and stir over medium-high heat to boiling.

2. Clip a candy thermometer to the side of the pan. Cook over medium heat, without stirring, to 265 degrees—about 40 minutes. At this point the candy should be at the hard-ball stage, which

can be tested by quickly dipping out a small amount of the candy and dropping it into cold water. Then, with your fingers form a small ball of the candy. It will be at the hard-ball stage if it does not flatten until pressed.

3. Remove the saucepan from the heat. Stir in the margarine. Stir in the flavoring and coloring, if desired.

4. Pour into a 15×10×1-inch greased pan. Cool for 15 to 20 minues, or until easy to handle.

5. Divide the candy into 4 pieces. Twist and pull each piece until it turns a creamy color (about 10 minutes). The candy is ready if it cracks when tapped on the counter.

6. With buttered scissors, cut the taffy into bite-size pieces. Wrap in clear plastic wrap.

Makes about 1 1/2 pounds (48 servings)

Salt is physiologically absolutely necessary for human life, equal in importance to water, and they must be maintained in a strict ratio to each other in the body.

Salted Crackers

> 2 cups all-purpose flour
> $1/_2$ cup granulated sugar
> $1/_4$ cup butter or margarine
> 1 egg
> $3/_4$ teaspoon baking soda
> 2 teaspoons water
> $1/_2$ cup butter, melted
> Salt

1. Preheat the oven to 350 degrees.

2. Put the flour and sugar in a medium-size bowl. Cut in the butter until crumbly. Make a well in the center.

3. Beat the egg until frothy.

4. Dissolve the soda in the water in a small container and add to the egg. Pour the egg mixture into the well in the flour mixture. Stir to make a firm batter. If too stiff, add water, but only 1 small spoonful at a time.

5. Roll thin on a lightly floured surface. Cut into rounds or squares. Pierce with a fork. Brush with melted butter and sprinkle with salt.

6. Bake on a greased baking sheet for about 15 minutes, or until golden.

Makes 5 to 6 dozen small crackers

Salmon on Salt

Kosher salt
4 center-cut salmon fillets, each about $^1/_2$ pound, skin on (but scaled)

1. Heat a 12-inch nonstick skillet over high heat for about 5 minutes. Cover the skillet with $^1/_4$ inch salt. Heat until the salt starts to turn brown.

2. Add the salmon, skin side down. Cook over high heat about 5 minutes, or until well browned on the bottom.

3. Cover the skillet with the lid for 1 minute longer (more if you like it well-done). Cooking for 6 minutes renders the salmon medium-rare; cook longer for well-done.

Makes 4 servings

Black Sea Bass Baked in Salt

1 black sea bass (1³/₄ pounds), cleaned
Coarsely ground black pepper to taste
5 pounds kosher salt
2 tablespoons extra virgin olive oil
Lemons for garnish

1. Preheat the oven to 400 degrees.

2. Season the cavity of the rinsed and dried fish with pepper.

3. Spread 2 pounds of the salt in the bottom of a 13×9×2-inch baking dish. Press the fish lightly into the salt. Pour the remaining salt on top of the fish to cover it completely. Sprinkle the salt with water to help form a crust. Use the palm of your hand to pat down the surface, following the shape of the fish. Bake in the center of the oven for 25 minutes. (If you prefer your fish well-done, add 5 minutes to the cooking time.)

4. Remove the fish and let sit for 3 minutes.

5. Beginning at the side, carefully break the salt crust and discard the salt. Gently lift the fish to a cutting board with a long spatula. Fillet the fish and transfer to a platter.

6. Drizzle with olive oil and sprinkle with coarsely ground black pepper. Serve immediately garnished with lemon halves.

Serves 2

The U.S. government is investigating the possibility of storing radioactive waste in underground salt mines. It has been suggested that their dryness, ability to withstand earthquakes, and 800-degree melting point make salt deposits the safest nuclear graveyards.

Whole Chicken Baked in Salt

$^1/_4$ cup white wine
1 roasting chicken ($3^1/_2$ to 4 pounds)
1 piece (2 inches) ginger root, cut into small
*   pieces*
1 lemon cut into 8 pieces
3 scallions coarsely chopped
4 pounds (coarse) salt

1. Rub half of the wine into the center of the chicken and place the ginger, lemon, and scallions into the cavity of the chicken. Tie the legs together. Rub the remaining wine over the outside of the chicken and let stand until the skin dries.

2. Wrap the chicken in a double thickness of cheesecloth, tying the ends over the breast.

3. Heat the salt in a large wok over high heat, stirring frequently until the salt is hot to touch (7 to 10 minutes). Remove all of the salt to a bowl except for a 1-inch layer in the bottom of the wok.

4. Place the chicken, breast up, on top of the salt in

the wok and cover it completely with the remaining salt. Cover the wok and cook the chicken over medium-low heat for 2 hours. Test for doneness by scraping away the salt near a thigh and piercing it with a knife to see if the juices run clear.

5. When the chicken is fully cooked, lift it out of the wok by the cheesecloth, transfer to a serving platter, and carve immediately.

Makes 4 servings

Strangely enough, while common salt is essential to life, the elements that make up salt, if found alone, are deadly. Sodium is a metal that bursts into flame when it comes into contact with water, and chlorine is a gas that in its pure form is deadly to both plants and animals.

Spiced Salt

Spice up your favorite salty snacks such as popcorn with this Caribbean treat.

1 tablespoon salt
1/4 teaspoon five-spice powder
1 teaspoon toasted and ground peppercorns

1. Mix all the ingredients well.

2. Store in an airtight container for use anytime.

Herbed Salt

This is another popular salt blend to spice up such things as baked potatoes or to try as the popular topping for fried plantain bananas, as they do in the Caribbean.

1/2 teaspoon dried oregano
1/2 teaspoon dried thyme
1/2 teaspoon garlic powder
1/2 teaspoon salt

1. Mix all the ingredients well.

2. Store in an airtight container for use anytime.

Fried Plantains Topped with Herbed Salt

1 or 2 large plantains
Vegetable oil
Herbed salt (see recipe above)

1. Cut the plantains into $1/2$-inch slices.

2. Pour $1/2$ inch oil into a heavy skillet and heat to 325 degrees.

3. Add the plantains and fry until soft (about 2 minutes per side). Transfer with a slotted spoon to a paper towel.

4. Just before serving, reheat the oil to 375 degrees.

5. Use a meat pounder or another heavy object to flatten the plantains to the thinness of potato chips.

6. Refry the plantains until golden (about 1 minute per side).

7. Sprinkle with herbed salt and serve.

Toasted Pumpkin Seeds

Seeds of 1 pumpkin
2 tablespoons vegetable oil
Salt to taste

1. Rinse the pumpkin seeds to remove all of the pulp and pat dry with paper towels. Let stand for several hours to dry.

2. Preheat the oven to 375 degrees.

3. Toss the seeds with the oil and salt to taste. Bake the seeds in the oven, stirring occasionally, until golden brown, about 25 to 30 minutes.

4. Let cool completely and add more salt if needed.

Iodine is not the only substance added to salt in order to insure its widespread ingestion. In France, Mexico, and Switzerland, fluoride is added to salt to prevent dental problems. In Egypt, salt is fortified with iron.

Edamame *(Japanese Salted Soybeans)*

The Japanese have a very delicious and healthy snack that is terrific for setting out at parties or simply as a substitute for the popcorn or chips you are accustomed to eating while watching videos at home. Bags of frozen soybeans can be found at any specialty Asian grocery store.

> *1 bag frozen soybeans*
> *Salt*

1. Add the soybeans to a pot of boiling water and boil for 5 minutes, or until tender. Drain well.

2. Put the soybeans into a bowl and generously salt.

3. Eat the soybeans by simply popping the beans out of the pods into your mouth, then discard the pods into another bowl.

Coarse Salt Breadsticks

$1/4$-ounce package ($2^1/2$ teaspoons) active dry
   yeast
$1^1/2$ teaspoons sugar
$3/4$ cup lukewarm water
$2^1/2$ to 3 cups all-purpose flour
1 teaspoon table salt
$1/4$ cup olive oil
Cornmeal for sprinkling baking sheets
1 slightly beaten egg white
1 tablespoon water
Coarse salt

1. In a large bowl, mix the yeast with $1/2$ teaspoon of the sugar and add the lukewarm water, stirring for 5 minutes or until foamy.

2. Add the remaining teaspoon sugar, 2 cups of the flour, the salt, and the oil, and beat until combined.

3. Knead the dough, adding enough flour to form a ball, and then knead the dough for 5 minutes until soft but not sticky. Cover the dough with a kitchen towel for 15 minutes.

4. Divide the dough into 12 pieces (keeping them all covered, except for the piece you are working with). Roll the dough between your palms to form 14-inch ropes and arrange 2 inches apart on a baking sheet. Sprinkle with cornmeal.

5. Let the breadsticks rise, covered loosely, in a warm place for about 40 minutes.

6. Preheat the oven to 450 degrees. Combine the egg white and 1 tablespoon water. Brush the breadsticks lightly with the mixture and sprinkle with coarse salt.

7. Bake the breadsticks in the middle of the oven for 12 to 15 minutes, or until pale golden, then let cool on a rack for 12 minutes.

Makes 12 breadsticks

By weight people are 70 percent fluid, the same percentage as the earth's surface that is covered by ocean. The sea within each of us has the same salinity as the Precambrian seas of three billion years ago.

Salty Pretzels

$4^1/_2$ cups all-purpose flour
1 package active dry yeast
$1^1/_2$ cups milk
$^1/_4$ cup sugar
2 tablespoons cooking oil
2 tablespoons plus 1 teaspoon salt
3 quarts boiling water
1 slightly beaten egg white
1 tablespoon water
Coarse salt

1. In a mixing bowl, stir together $1^1/_2$ cups of the flour and the yeast.

2. In a saucepan, heat and stir the milk, sugar, oil, and 1 teaspoon of the salt until warm. Add to the flour mixture. Beat with an electric mixer on a low speed for 30 seconds, scraping the bowl constantly. Beat on high speed for 3 minutes. Using a spoon, stir in as much of the remaining flour as you can.

3. Place the mixture on a lightly floured surface. Knead in enough of the remaining flour to make

a moderately stiff dough that is smooth and elastic. Shape the dough into a ball. Place the dough in a greased bowl and turn once to grease the surface. Cover and let rise in a warm place until double its original size, about $1^1/_2$ hours.

4. Punch the dough down. Turn out onto a lightly floured surface. Cover and let rest 10 minutes. Roll the dough into a 12×10-inch rectangle. Cut into twenty 12×$^1/_2$-inch strips. Gently pull each strip into a rope about 16 inches long.

5. Shape each pretzel by crossing one end over the other to form a circle, overlapping about 4 inches on each end. Take one end of the dough in each hand and twist once at the point where the dough overlaps. Lift each end across to the edge of the circle opposite it and tuck them under the edges to make a traditional pretzel shape. Moisten the ends and press to seal.

6. Place the pretzels on a greased baking sheet. Bake in the oven at 475 degrees for 4 minutes. Remove from the oven and lower the temperature to 350 degrees.

7. Dissolve the remaining 2 tablespoons of salt in the boiling water. Lower the pretzels into the

boiling water. Boil for 2 minutes, turning once. Remove with a slotted spoon and drain on a paper towel. Let stand for a few seconds before placing about $1/2$ inch apart on well-greased baking sheets.

8. Combine the egg white and 1 tablespoon water. Brush the pretzels with the mixture. Sprinkle lightly with the coarse salt. Bake at 350 degrees for 25 minutes, or until golden brown. Cool the pretzels on a wire rack.

Makes 20 pretzels

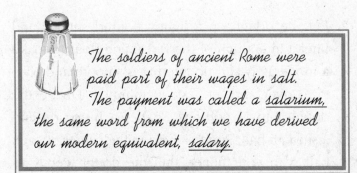

The soldiers of ancient Rome were paid part of their wages in salt. The payment was called a _salarium_, the same word from which we have derived our modern equivalent, _salary_.

Salt Bagels

4 3/4 cups all-purpose flour
1 package active dry yeast
1 1/2 cups warm water
1/4 cup sugar
1 teaspoon salt
1 slightly beaten egg white
6 cups water, for boiling
1 tablespoon water
Coarse salt

1. Combine 2 cups of the flour and the yeast. Add the warm water, 3 tablespoons of the sugar, and 1 teaspoon salt. Beat with an electric mixer on low speed for 30 seconds. Beat on high speed for 3 minutes. Using a spoon, stir in as much remaining flour as you can.

2. Put the dough on a lightly floured surface and knead in enough of the remaining flour to make a moderately stiff dough that is smooth and elastic. Cover and let rest 20 minutes. Divide the dough into 12 portions. Shape each portion into a smooth ball. Punch a hole in the center of each ball with your finger. Pull the dough gently to

make a 2-inch hole, keeping the bagel uniformly shaped. Place on a greased baking sheet. Cover and let rise for 20 minutes.

3. Broil the raised bagels about 5 inches from the heat for 3 to 4 minutes, turning once. Meanwhile, bring 6 cups water and the remaining 1 table-spoon of sugar to a boil. Reduce the heat and simmer the bagels for 7 minutes, turning once. Drain on paper towels.

4. Combine the egg white and 1 tablespoon water. Brush the bagels with the egg mixture. Sprinkle lightly with coarse salt. Bake in a 375-degree oven for 25 to 30 minutes, or until the tops are golden brown.

Makes 12 bagels

In ancient Greece, slaves were bought and sold for salt. The practice of buying and selling slaves for salt was the reason behind the origin of the phrase, "He's not worth his salt."

Salty Pickles

One of the most delicious salty treats is a crisp pickle. But pickles, in fact, come in many forms, and pickled cucumbers are just the starting point for pickle lovers. Local grocery stores are now carrying everything from pickled green beans to pickled okra. And almost just as fun as eating pickles is making them yourself. While canning the old-fashioned way can be quite a lengthy and involved process requiring meticulous attention to hygienic methods, there are some quick and easy recipes for pickles that I've found that are fun to make and yield delicious results.

The amount of salt in the oceans alone is estimated to be more than 100 million times mankind's annual needs.

Gone-in-a-Second Pickles

3 pounds cucumbers
6 tablespoons salt
1^1/$_2$ cups boiling water
2 tablespoons sugar
^{1}/$_2$ tablespoon Accent
6 cloves garlic, sliced
^{1}/$_4$ cup vinegar
1^1/$_2$ cups ice water
2 teaspoons dried red pepper flakes

1. Cut the cucumbers in half lengthwise, then slice diagonally into ^{1}/$_2$-inch slices and place in a large bowl.

2. Mix the salt with the boiling water and pour over the cucumbers. Let stand 1 hour, then drain.

3. Mix the remaining ingredients and pour over the cucumbers and refrigerate.

Makes 15 servings

Freezer Pickles

3 quarts sliced cucumbers
3 cups chopped celery
1 large onion, sliced
2 green bell peppers, cut in strips
1 head cauliflower, cut into bite-size pieces
6 medium carrots, sliced
1/4 cup salt
4 cups sugar
6 cups vinegar

1. Mix together all the ingredients except for the sugar and vinegar; let stand overnight. Drain.

2. Boil the sugar and vinegar. Cool. Pour over the vegetables.

3. Freeze in plastic containers. Thaw at room temperature to use. These pickles are ready to eat immediately.

Makes about 8 quarts

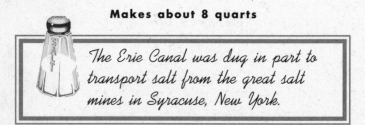

The Erie Canal was dug in part to transport salt from the great salt mines in Syracuse, New York.

Sunomomo *Dressing for Cucumbers*

3 medium cucumbers, sliced
$1/2$ cup rice vinegar
$1/4$ cup fresh lemon juice
1 teaspoon salt
1 teaspoon freshly grated ginger
$1/4$ teaspoon wasabi *(powdered horseradish)*
    dissolved in 1 teaspoon water
2 to 4 tablespoons sugar

1. Place the cucumber slices on paper towels to drain any excess liquid. Wrap in paper towels and refrigerate until serving time.

2. Combine all dressing ingredients in a small bowl, adding sugar to taste. Stir until the sugar and *wasabi* are dissolved.

3. At serving time, place the cucumbers in a bowl, pour on the dressing, and toss.

Makes 6 servings

Quick Turnip Pickles (*Kabu no Sokuseki-zuke*)

An example of instant salt pickling. It takes only an hour for these pickles to ripen, and they will keep, covered, in the refrigerator for the better part of a week. Also appropriate for cucumbers sliced in thin wafers. Peel and seed large cucumbers.

> *12 medium turnips*
> *5 heaping tablespoons salt*
> *4 pieces* **kombu** *(giant kelp)*
> *1 square* **yuzu** *citron (lemon rind)*

1. Cut off the greens from the turnips and save. Wash the turnips, peel, then cut into very fine julienne strips. Wash the greens, dry, then chop finely.

2. Put the turnip strips and finely chopped greens into a bowl and sprinkle with salt. Table salt is fine. Knead with your hands and mix thoroughly to draw the water out of the vegetables. In less than a minute, a fair amount of liquid will be produced. Discard this liquid.

3. Add the *kombu* and *yuzu* citron (or use a 1-inch square of lemon rind). Let stand, covered and with a light weight on the lid, for 1 hour at room temperature.

4. Pick out a portion from the bowl with chopsticks or a fork and shake off the liquid. Arrange in a mound on individual pickle dishes. You may season with a few drops of soy sauce, if desired.

Makes 15 servings

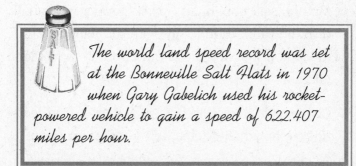

The world land speed record was set at the Bonneville Salt Flats in 1970 when Gary Gabelich used his rocket-powered vehicle to gain a speed of 622.407 miles per hour.

Indian Sweet Lemon Pickles

9 lemons
4 tablespoons coarse or kosher salt
1$^{1}/_{2}$ tablespoons cumin seeds, toasted and
  ground
1 tablespoon coarsely ground black pepper
3 cups sugar
2 tablespoons seedless raisins
8 dried hot red peppers

1. Wash the lemons in cold water and dry thoroughly.

2. Quarter 6 of the lemons from the top almost all the way through to the bottom, leaving about $^{1}/_{2}$ inch so they'll hold together. Squeeze the juice from the other lemons.

3. Mix the salt, cumin, and black pepper in a small dish, and mix thoroughly with the lemons. Stuff the lemons into a quart jar and pour in the lemon juice.

4. Cover with cheesecloth to prevent dirt from getting in the jar, and let sit in the open for about 1 week.

5. On the seventh day, pour the juices from the jar into an enamel or stainless steel pan, add the sugar, and cook over low heat, stirring until the sugar dissolves. Add the lemons and cook, stirring gently, for 8 minutes or so. Stir in the raisins and peppers. Put the lemons in a sterilized jar and seal the lid. Let sit for a week or so before eating. Use as you would any pickle, as an accompaniment.

Makes 1 quart

Only one pound of salt is required to melt forty-six pounds of ice at thirty-degrees Fahrenheit. This is why salt is so elemental in clearing roads in winter.

Japanese Pickled Cauliflower— with Cola

1 medium cauliflower, separated into florets,
    washed and drained
1 medium green bell pepper, washed, cored,
    seeded, and cut into 2-inch strips
Water
$^1/_2$ cup very thinly sliced celery
$^3/_4$ cup cola
6 tablespoons wine vinegar or white vinegar
$^1/_4$ cup sugar
$1^1/_2$ teaspoons salt

1. In a large bowl, combine the cauliflower florets and bell pepper strips. Cover with boiling water. Let stand for 2 minutes, then drain thoroughly. Add the celery.

2. In a small pan, heat the cola, wine vinegar, sugar, and salt. Pour over the vegetables. Toss lightly with a fork.

3. Pack into a 1-quart glass jar. Push down lightly so the liquid covers the vegetables. Cover and chill overnight. This will keep for several days if refrigerated.

Makes about 1 quart

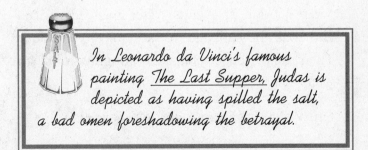

In Leonardo da Vinci's famous painting The Last Supper, Judas is depicted as having spilled the salt, a bad omen foreshadowing the betrayal.

Korean Kimchi

Kimchi is a very spicy Korean pickled dish that comes in many varieties. It has a very dense garlic flavor, so if you are a garlic lover, this is a recipe you should definitely try.

> *3 pounds Chinese cabbage*
> *4 cups water*
> *2 cups salt*
> *$^{1}/_{2}$ carrot*
> *2 red bell peppers, seeded*
> *$^{1}/_{2}$ large green onion*
> *1 small bulb garlic (8 to 10 cloves)*
> *2 tablespoons fresh ginger, grated*
> *1 tablespoon sugar*
> *1 tablespoon salt*

1. Cut the cabbages lengthwise into 4 sections. Make a brine of 4 cups water and 2 cups salt, and soak the cabbage in the liquid for 8 hours. Then rinse the cabbage thoroughly in clean water and drain.

2. Finely shred the carrot and red peppers.

3. Mince the green onion, crush the garlic, and grate the ginger. Mix in a bowl with the carrot and pepper. Stir in the sugar and salt and mix well.

4. Pack the seasoning mixture between each leaf of the cabbage and put the stuffed cabbage in a large crock or jar. Press down and cover with plastic wrap, then place a heavy weight on top of the crock or jar.

5. Store at 65 to 70 degrees for 4 to 5 days. The kimchi is then ready to eat.

6. Remove one section at a time, cutting into serving-size pieces.

Makes 4 quarts

Annual salt production has increased over the past century from 10 million tons to 190 million tons.

SALT MUSEUMS AND OTHER INTERESTING SALT SITES AROUND THE WORLD

*B*ecause salt has played such a large part in the history of many communities and the mineral itself is of such vital importance, a number of salt museums have been created around the world. Each is fascinating both for the history of the region it represents and for its own history of salt and what that museum has chosen to include. If you can't make it to a particular region, with the Worldwide Web you can always visit these museums in cyberspace, since they all have their own sites.

Deutsches Salzmuseum (German Salt Museum), Lüneburg, Germany.

http://www.members.aol.com/saltmuseum/index.html

Lüneburg is known as "the city of salt" in northern Germany, and salt was produced here continuously for over one thousand years, until 1980. The salt museum calls itself a "hands-on" museum where visitors can see firsthand what the production of salt involved and also see some of the fascinating details of salt production through the ages.

DEUTSCHES SALZMUSEUM
Industrial Monument Saltworks of Lüneburg
Sulfmeisterstrasse 1
D-21335 Lüneburg
Germany
Phone: 49 4131 45065
FAX: 49 4131 45069
Open from May–September
Tours Monday–Friday, 11:00 A.M. & 3:00 P.M.;
Sunday, 3:00 p.m.

The Lion Salt Works Trust, Northwich, Cheshire, England.

http://www.iway.fr/sc/tribune/articles/uksalt/html

The Lion Salt Works was the last surviving UK saltworks to produce white salt by evaporation. It was built and operated by the same family from 1899 to its closing in 1986. The site is currently being restored through a trust and will be a museum dedicated to understanding the production of salt and its regional importance. A leaflet is available on the site, as is a quarterly newsletter documenting the progress of the work. Both can be obtained by writing:

Andrew Fielding, Director
THE LION SALT WORKS TRUST
Ollershaw Lane, Marston
Northwich
Cheshire, CW9 6ES
England
Phone/Fax: 44 1606 41823

The Salt Museum, Liverpool, New York
http://www.syracuse.ny.us/activities/features/salt.html

This museum illustrates the history of the Onondaga salt industry and sits on the site of the original boiling block where salt was made. Through artifacts, photos, and changing exhibitions, visitors can learn the story of how Syracuse once supplied the United States with salt.

SALT MUSEUM
PO Box 146

Liverpool, NY 13088
Phone: 315-453-6767
FAX: 315-453-6762
Open from May–September.
Hours are Tuesday–Sunday, noon–5:00 P.M.

The Salt Museum, Northwich, Cheshire, England
http://www.liverpool.com/frodsham/places/salt.html

This small and friendly museum is housed in the old workhouse in Northwich. Included are displays on mining, work conditions, and a history of the salt industry in the area. The museum lies just a half mile south of the center of Northwich.

SALT MUSEUM
162 Condon Road
Northwich
Cheshire, CW9 8AB
England
Phone: 44 1696 41331
Open year-round.
Hours are Tuesday–Friday, 10:00 A.M.–5:00 P.M.

Tobacco and Salt Museum, Tokyo, Japan
http://www.jtnet.ad.jp/www/jt/museum/map.html

Being an island nation with almost no natural salt deposits of its own, Japan has had great difficulty and gone to great expense trying to obtain salt over the ages. Salt is very cumbersome and expensive to import, and with no land that could provide any saltworks, the shipping and import costs have been tremendous. Japan has thus been developing, at great cost, its own systems of obtaining salt through seawater. The salt section of the tobacco and salt museum is devoted to the quest for their own production and their means of obtaining salt over the ages.

TOBACCO AND SALT MUSEUM
1-16-8 Jinnan
Shibuya-ku, Tokyo
Japan
Phone: 81 3 3476 2041
Fax: 81 3 3476 5692
Open year-round.
Hours are Tuesday–Sunday, 10:00 A.M.–
6:00 P.M.

Wieliczka Salt Mine, Poland

http://places4u.com/en/vac4u/poland/wonders.html

One of the oldest and surely the most fantastic of all salt mines, Wieliczka lies only about twenty miles from Kraków. Because of its fantastic sculptures carved out of the salt, in 1978 the mine was placed on UNESCO's list of world-class landmarks of cultural and natural heritage and is listed among the top twelve attractions of the world. Over the ages it has been visited by thousands, including Copernicus, Goethe, Baden-Powell, and Pope John Paul II.

WIELICZKA SALT MINE

14 km southeast of Kraców, near Route 4 (E22)

Phone: 48-12-78-26-53

FAX: 48-12-78-62-32

Open year-round.

Hours are daily from April 16–October 15, 8 A.M.–6 P.M., and daily from October 16–April 15, from 8 a.m.–to 4 P.M.

Salzburg-Bad Durrnberg Salt Mine

http://www.austria.eu.net/image/salz/mines.html

This salt mine is one of the oldest centers of alpine salt production in the world. Throughout history, this mine brought great riches to the area, so the salt, because of the wealth it provided, was referred to as "white gold." The mine tours include tram rides through deep tunnels and a boat ride on the subterranean salt lake. Nearby is a reconstructed Celtic village detailing the area's rich history.

> SALZBURG-BAD DURRNBERG SALT MINE
> Phone: 43 6245 83511 15
> Hours are April 1–October 31, 9 A.M.–5 P.M.
> November 1–January 6, 11 A.M.–3 P.M.
> February 2–March 31, 11 A.M.–3 p.m.
> Closed January 7–February 1.

Bad Ischl Salt Mine

http://www.austria.eu.net/image/salz/mines.html

Set next to a fantastic local health resort, Bad Ischl Salt Mine is set deep within an amazing alpine mountain. Mine tours include a deep descent into the mountain via mining trams to the mysterious salt lake situated in the cavernous depths.

BAD ISCHL MINE
Phone: 43 6132 23948 31
Hours are May 1–June 30, 9:00 A.M.–3:45 P.M.
July 1–August 31, 10:00 A.M.–4:45 P.M.
September 1–September 21, 9 A.M.–3:45 P.M.
Closed September 22–April 30.

Hallstatt Salt Mine

http://www.austria.eu.net/image/salz/mines.html

One of the oldest salt mines in the world, Hallstatt Mine provides a re-creation of its ancient history in the mine tours. From the ancient pinewood spills preserved in the mine tunnels since 1000 B.C. to the location of the "Man in Salt," who was found over three hundred years ago, visitors see the past brought to life. Tours include mine tram rides into the depths of the mountain to the deep salt lake.

HALLSTATT SALT MINE
Phone: 43 6134 8251 72
Hours are April 1–October 26, 9:30 A.M.–3 P.M.

May 25–September 15, 9:30 A.M.–4:30 P.M.
September 16–October 26, 9:30 A.M.–3 P.M.
Closed October 27–March 31.

Altaussee Salt Mine

http://www.austria.eu.net/image/salt/mines.html

Often referred to as "Europe's Treasure Vault," the Altaussee Salt Mine was where many of Europe's cultural artifacts were protected during World War II. From its famous chapel dedicated to Saint Barbara to its stunning subterranean salt lake, Altaussee Salt Mine is one of the most beautiful salt mines in Austria, and the tour provides a fascinating walk through history.

ALTAUSSEE SALT MINE
Phone: 43 3622 71332
Open year-round.
Hours are daily 10 A.M.–4 P.M.

Bonneville Salt Flats

The Bonneville Salt Flats are an otherworldly looking expanse of land stretching across Utah for many miles. They were formed when a great Pleistocene-era lake, which rivaled Lake Michigan in size, evaporated.

The first white man to cross the flats was Jedediah Smith in 1827. Six years later, the flats were explored and mapped by Joseph Reddeford, who was working on behalf of Captain Benjamin Bonneville, for whom the salt flats are now named.

In 1845 John Frémont and his expedition crossed through the salt flats in an attempt to find a shorter overland route to the Pacific Coast. The route later became known as Fremont's Cutoff, and this cutoff would be a factor in the tragedy for the Donner-Reed party in 1846. Trying to speed their journey, the Donner-Reed party attempted to cross the flats, but they experienced a great delay when their wagons became mired in the mud just below the surface of the salt crust. Because of this great delay they arrived at the pass in the Sierra Nevada mountains only to find it blocked by snow. Forced to camp in the area, they soon found themselves faced with the threat of starvation. Seventeen members then attempted to cross the pass on snowshoes and only seven survived to bring in relief parties. When the relief parties came in, only forty of the original eighty-seven in the party were still alive. Death by starvation for some of these forty was averted only by their resorting to cannibalism. After the Donner-Reed tragedy, the cutoff was little used by westward migrators.

It wasn't until fifty years later that the area was first conceived of as a raceway. William Randolph Hearst, in a publicity stunt, hired William Rishel of Cheyenne, Wyoming, to attempt a crossing on bicycle, which took the cyclist twenty-two hours. Since that time, hundreds of land speed records have been set and broken in both motorcycle and automobile races.

In 1949 the hot rodders of America began a tradition of yearly meets that continues today. The Bonneville Opener is held in July of each year, and the World of Speed is held each September. Thousands of visitors, auto racers, and filmmakers make the Bonneville Salt Flats a world-famous destination.

The Bonneville Salt Flats are located north of Interstate Highway 80 near Wendover, Utah. For information contact:

BUREAU OF LAND MANAGEMENT SALT LAKE FIELD
    OFFICE
2370 South 2300 West
Salt Lake City, Utah 84119
Phone: 801-977-4300

BIBLIOGRAPHY

Baking Soda Bonanza, Peter Ciullo. New York: Harper-Collins, 1995.

Better Homes and Gardens New Cook Book, Jennifer Darling, Linda Henry, Rosemary C. Hutchinson, Mary Major. Iowa: Meredith Corporation, 1989.

Company's Coming, Jean Pare. Alberta, CA: Company's Coming Ltd., 1983.

The Complete Book of Superstition, Prophecy and Luck, Leonard R. N. Ashley. New York: Barricade Books, 1984.

Crystals from the Sea: A Look at Salt, A. Harris Stone and Dale Ingmanson. New Jersey: Prentice Hall, 1969.

Crystals of Life: The Story of Salt, Robert Kraske. New York: Doubleday, 1968.

A Dictionary of Superstitions, Sophia Lasne and Andre Pascal Gaultier. New Jersey: Prentice Hall, 1984.

A Dictionary of Superstitions, Iona Opie and Moira Tatem. New York: Oxford University Press, 1989.

Extraordinary Origins of Everyday Things, Charles Panati. New York: Harper & Row, 1987.

The Family Guide to Natural Medicine, Reader's Digest Association. New York: Reader's Digest, 1993.

The First Book of Salt, Olive Burt. New York: Franklin Watts, 1965.

Guide to Natural Medicine, Reader's Digest Association. New York: Reader's Digest, 1993.

Household Hints and Healthy Tips, Reader's Digest Association. New York: Reader's Digest, 1988.

Keep the Buttered Side Up: Food Superstitions from Around the World, Kathlyn Gay. New York: Walker & Company, 1995.

99 Ways to a Simple Lifestyle, Center for Science in the Public Interest. New York: Anchor Press, 1977.

Poisons and Antidotes, Carol Turkington. New York: Facts on File, 1994.

Practical Problem Solver, Reader's Digest Association. New York: Reader's Digest, 1992.

Salt Institute Web Site. www.saltinstitute.org.

"Salt: The Essence of Life," Gordon Young. Washington, D.C.: *National Geographic Magazine,* September 1977.

The Science of Salt, Fobert Froman. New York: David McKay, 1967.

Stories Behind Everyday Things, Reader's Digest Association. New York: Reader's Digest, 1993.

The Story of Superstition, Philip Waterman. New York: Alfred Knopf, 1929.

Index